Tricycle Theatre presents

A BOY AND HIS SOUL

By
Colman Domingo

9/2/14

ABOUT THE TRICYCLE THEATRE

The Tricycle views the world through a variety of lenses, bringing unheard voices into the mainstream. It presents high quality and innovative work, which provokes debate and emotionally engages. Located in Brent, the most diverse borough in London, the Tricycle is a local venue with an international vision.

Converted from a music and dance hall, the Tricycle opened in 1980 as the permanent home of the Wakefield Tricycle Company – a touring theatre company which presented new plays and children's theatre throughout Britain and internationally. Ironically, they never played Wakefield.

Today, with Indhu Rubasingham as Artistic Director, the Tricycle Theatre continues its reputation for world-class British and international work, reflecting the exceptional diversity of its local community.

Open seven days a week, the Tricycle has a unique 235 seat theatre, an independent 300 seat cinema, a vibrant bar and café, plus three rehearsal spaces which are used for our productions, workshops and Creative Learning projects.

Recent productions include *Red Velvet*, which launched Indhu Rubasingham's inaugural season and returns to the Tricycle in 2014 prior to a New York transfer; *The Arabian Nights*, a modern re-imagining of ancient tales for young people; and *Paper Dolls*, an extraordinary true story of cultures colliding in Tel Aviv which was developed with The Sundance Institute Theatre Program. We have also recently co-produced with Shared Experience, and collaborated with Tiata Fahodzi, Liverpool Everyman and Playhouse Theatres, and Eclipse Theatre.

CINEMA

Our luxury 300 seat cinema shows the best art-house and mainstream films alongside festivals and special Q&A screenings.

> *"This King of Kilburn is a sleek and stylish single-screen gem that attracts moviegoers from all over London"*
> The Guardian

Highlights include our Q&As with acclaimed writers and directors, such as Moira Buffini, Dominic Dromgoole, Stephen Frears, Mike Leigh and Ken Loach, and with renowned actors including Jim Broadbent, Kim Cattrall, Paul Chahidi, Julie Christie, Glenda Jackson, Simon Paisley Day and Rosamund Pike.

Recent partners include: NT Live; Globe on Screen; BFI London Film Festival; Images of Black Women Film Festival; the UK Jewish Film Festival; DocHouse; Kilburn Film Festival.

The Tricycle is a hub where cultures connect, creativity can flourish and curiosity is engendered.

CREATIVE LEARNING

The Tricycle's Creative Learning programme works to develop the imaginations, aspirations and potential of children and young people in the diverse community of Brent and beyond. Collaborating with schools and young people, we use theatre, drama and film, to bring unheard young voices into the mainstream; creating work that engages the emotions and provokes debate. Whether as audiences, writers, performers or producers of new work at the theatre, young people are at the Tricycle's heart.

For more information about our current workshops and social inclusion projects, please visit www.tricycle.co.uk/young-people

Tricycle Theatre presents

A BOY AND HIS SOUL

Written and performed by	Colman Domingo
Director	Titas Halder
Designer	Richard Kent
Lighting Designer	Oliver Fenwick
Sound Designer	Mike Thacker
Production Manager	Shaz McGee
Company Stage Manager	Louise Green
Sound Operator	Rosie Horan
Set Construction	Ben Jones
Chief LX	Max Blackman
Crew	Paul Kizintas
	Devika Ramcharan
	Scott Carter

Indhu would like to express her gratitude to Sundance Theatre Institute, through whom she met Colman. Without them, this collaboration might not have happened.

The Tricycle would also like to thank Jamie Martin, Michael Prosser and Monique Quesada from the US Embassy who have helped in bringing this project to fruition.

A Boy and His Soul was first produced by the VINEYARD THEATRE, Douglas Aibel, Artistic Director, New York City

A Boy And His Soul is produced by special arrangement with THE GERSH AGENCY, 41 Madison Avenue, 33rd Floor, New York, NY 10010.

COLMAN DOMINGO
Writer & Performer
Colman Domingo is a Tony Award-nominated and Obie award-winning actor, playwright and director. For theatre, his work includes the original company of *The Scottsboro Boys*, which he will reprise later this year at the Young Vic. Other theatre work includes *Passing Strange* and *Chicago* (Broadway). For film, his forthcoming credits include Lee Daniel's *The Butler, All is Bright, A Long Walk, Hairbrained* and *Newlyweeds*. Other film work includes Steven Spielberg's *Lincoln*, Spike Lee's *Red Hook Summer* and *Passing Strange*. A Lucille Lortel Award-winning playwright, his play *Wild with Happy* recently premiered at The Public Theater in New York and Theatreworks in California. Domingo currently has a residency with People's Light and Theater Company and is under commission from Milwaukee Rep, The American Conservatory Theater and Inner Voices.

TITAS HALDER
Director
Titas Halder is a writer and director. He was previously Resident Assistant Director at the Donmar Warehouse, Creative Associate at the Bush Theatre and Literary Associate at the Finborough Theatre. As director, work includes *The Dance of Death* by August Strindberg/Conor McPherson (Donmar/Trafalgar Studios), *The Goat at Midnight* by Anne Carson (*Sixty Six Books* Bush Theatre), *Painting a Wall* by David Lan (Finborough Theatre), *Write to Rock* (Clwyd Theatr Cymru). Writing includes *Not Cricket* (Paines Plough), *Darkling* (Prithvi Theatre/Paines Plough), *Replica* (Nabokov).
Titas was also Assistant Director on the Tricycle productions *Red Velvet* and *Stones in his Pockets*.

RICHARD KENT
Designer
Upcoming work includes: *Handbagged* (Tricycle).
Theatre includes: *Paper Dolls* (Tricycle), *The Dance of Death* (Trafalgar Studios); *Josephine Hart Poetry Week* (ARTS); *Macbeth* (Sheffield Crucible); *13* (NYMT, Apollo); *Clockwork* (Hightide Festival); *Titanic – Scenes From The British Wreck Commissioners Inquiry: 1912* (MAC Theatre, Belfast); *Richard II* (Donmar Warehouse); *Mixed Marriage* (Finborough); *The Stronger & Pariah* (Arcola). Richard has worked as Associate to Christopher Oram since 2008, working on numerous shows at the Donmar Warehouse including: *Spelling Bee, King Lear* (also BAM, New York), *Passion, Red* (also Broadway and Mark Taper Forum, LA), *A Streetcar Named Desire* as well as *Ivanov, Twelfth Night, Madame De Sade*, (Donmar West End) and *Hamlet* (DWE, Elsinore Denmark and Broadway).
Work as Associate includes: *Don Giovanni* (Metropolitan Opera); *Madame Butterfly* (Houston Grand Opera); *Billy Budd, Le Nozze Di Figaro* (Glyndebourne); *Company* (Sheffield Crucible); *Danton's Death* (National); *Evita* (Broadway).

OLIVER FENWICK

Lighting Designer

Upcoming work includes: *Handbagged* (Tricycle)

Theatre includes: *Paper Dolls, Red Velvet, Poison* and *The Caretaker* (Tricycle); *Bracken Moor* (Tricycle/Shared Experience); *The Holy Rosenbergs, Happy Now?* (National Theatre); *Routes, The Witness, Disconnect* (Royal Court); *My City, Ruined* (Almeida); *The Winter's Tale, The Taming Of The Shrew, Julius Caesar, The Drunks, The Grain Store* (RSC); *Berenice, Huis Clos* (Donmar); *After Miss Julie* (Young Vic); *Saved, A Midsummer Night's Dream* (Lyric, Hammersmith); *To Kill A Mocking Bird, The Beggar's Opera* (Regent's Park Theatre); *The Madness Of George III, Ghosts, Kean, The Solid Gold Cadillac, Secret Rapture* (West End); *The Kitchen Sink, The Contingency Plan, If There Is I Haven't Found It Yet* (Bush Theatre); *A Number* (Chocolate Factory); *Private Lives, The Giant, Glass Eels, Comfort Me With Apples* (Hampstead); *Hamlet, The Caretaker, Comedy Of Errors* (Crucible Theatre, Sheffield).

MIKE THACKER

Sound Designer

Theatre designs include: *The Bloody Sunday Inquiry* (Tricycle/Tour), *Playboy of The West Indies* (Tricycle/Nottingham Playhouse) *Mary Rose* (Riverside Studios), *Ordinary Days* (Trafalgar Studios), *Everything Else Happened* (Edinburgh Festival). His operating work includes, *Jerry Springer the Opera* (Cambridge Theatre), *Chitty Chitty Bang Bang* (International Tour), *A Little Night Music* (Garrick Theatre), *End Of The Rainbow* (Trafalgar Studios) and currently *Top Hat* (UK Tour/Aldwych).

Mike has designed and operated plays and musicals all over the world.

Support Us

The Tricycle Theatre has always been a pioneer and a risk-taker. As we herald a new chapter, your support will help us to continue this bold tradition during uncertain economic times. Individuals, grant-making trusts and corporate partners play a vital role in supporting our ambitious artistic programme and creative learning work with young people in the local community.

'We believe deeply in all the work it does both artistically and educationally'
Primrose and David Bell, Tricycle members since 1996

With your support

- We can continue to push boundaries artistically across stage and screen, building on the success of productions such as the critically acclaimed and award-winning *Red Velvet* and *The Great Game: Afghanistan.*
- We can extend the reach of our creative learning programmes, inspiring a new generation of audiences and providing young theatre-makers with a professional context in which to develop their skills, aspirations and potential.

Join us today

'I like the atmosphere, like supporting the values of the Tricycle, and enjoy coming with friends.'
Steven Baruch, Tricycle member since 2004

Our members receive the very best benefits across stage and screen, with invitations to member events, priority booking, and opportunities to observe our creative learning work. Membership starts from just £125 per year. To join and for further details, please visit www.tricycle.co.uk/support, phone the Development Department on **020 7625 0132** or email **development@tricycle.co.uk**.

Thank you in advance for your support.

THANK YOU

We are extremely grateful to our supporters, whose help has made the work we produce at the Tricycle Theatre possible year after year. Thank you for your support.

PUBLIC FUNDING

TRUSTS AND FOUNDATIONS

FOYLE FOUNDATION   BackstageTrust

The Tricycle would also like to thank the Friends, Trailblazers and all anonymous donors.

Opportunities for corporate partnership include production sponsorship, funding a creative learning workshop, joining as a corporate member or supporting another element of the Tricycle's work on stage or screen, with benefits for both the company and staff. Please contact the Development Department on 020 7625 0132 for further details.

CORPORATE PARTNERS

Bloomberg

The Clancy Group PLC

Daniel & Harris Solicitors
J. Leon & Company Ltd
JPC Law
London Walks Ltd
Mulberry House School
The North London Tavern
Samuel French Ltd

We are enormously grateful to the members of our Development Committee, who volunteer their expertise and experience by advising on and supporting the Tricycle's fundraising activities.

Kay Ellen Consolver (Co-Chair); Judy Lever (Co-Chair); Lesley Adams; Nadhim Ahmed; Baz Bamigboye; Andrew Daniel; Sally Doganis; Grant Jones; Mairead Keohane; Jonathan Levy; Jeremy Lewison; Anneke Mendelsohn; Andree Molyneux; Allan Morgenthau; Michael Sandler; Christine Scholes; Caroline Schuck; Geraldine Sharpe-Newton; Sue Summers

The Tricycle Theatre was founded by Shirley Barrie and Ken Chubb.
The Tricycle Theatre Company Ltd. Registered Charity number 276892.
Registered Office: 269 Kilburn High Road, NW6 7JR
Administration: 020 7372 6611
Box Office: 020 7328 1000
Fax: 020 7328 0795
Email: info@tricycle.co.uk

A BOY AND HIS SOUL

Winner of the 2010 GLAAD Media Award
Outstanding New York Theater:
Broadway or Off Broadway Production

Winner of the 2010 Lucille Lortel Award
Outstanding Solo Show

Winner of the 2010 ITBA Award
Outstanding Solo Show

2010 Drama Desk Award Nomination
Outstanding Solo Performance

2010 Drama League Award Nomination
Distinguished Performance

A BOY AND HIS SOUL

A solo with soul music by
Colman Domingo

OBERON BOOKS
LONDON

WWW.OBERONBOOKS.COM

First published in 2013 by Oberon Books Ltd
521 Caledonian Road, London N7 9RH
Tel: +44 (0) 20 7607 3637 / Fax: +44 (0) 20 7607 3629
e-mail: info@oberonbooks.com
www.oberonbooks.com

A catalogue record for this book is available from the British
Library.

PB ISBN: 978-1-78319-058-4
E ISBN: 978-1-78319-557-2

Cover:
Photography by Kyle Zimmerman
Design by Rogers Eckersley Design
Courtesy of Vineyard Theatre

Printed, bound and converted
by CPI Group (UK) Ltd, Croydon, CR0 4YY.

Visit www.oberonbooks.com to read more about all our books
and to buy them. You will also find features, author interviews and
news of any author events, and you can sign up for e-newsletters
so that you're always first to hear about our new releases.

ABOUT THIS PLAY WITH SOUL MUSIC

A Boy and his Soul received several work in progress readings at the legendary jazz institution 55 Bar in Greenwich Village with indelible support from Ms. Queva Lutz in the summer of 2004. It was further developed in a workshop with Thick Description Theater Company in January 2005. *A Boy and his Soul* received its world premiere on July 1, 2005 at the Thick House in San Francisco produced by Thick Description under the direction of Tony Kelly. Scenic and Lighting design by Rick Martin. Costume by Raul Aktanov. Sound design by Colman Domingo and Tony Kelly. Music Compilation Colman Domingo and Clarence Bowles. *A Boy and his Soul* received a sold out revival production in honor of Thick Description's 20th Anniversary in September 2008. *A Boy and his Soul* premiered in New York to a sold-out house one-night-only event at Joe's Pub at the Public Theater on February 23, 2009. *A Boy and his Soul* opened the 2009-2010 season of The Vineyard Theater, Off Broadway, on September 24, 2009 directed by Tony Kelly, Choreography by Ken Roberson, Set Design by Rachel Hauck, Lighting Design by Marcus Doshi, Sound Design by Tom Morse and Costume Design by Toni Leslie James. Subsequent presentations have been presented at the OMAI festival for the University of Wisconsin/Madison and the Theater Development Fund.

Dramaturgy: Tony Kelly, Zack Willis, Lisa Ramirez, Leigh Fondakowski and Mark Wood.

Developmental Support: New York Theater Workshop, The Culture Project, New Professional Theater and the Theater Bay Area Cash Grant.

This play is dedicated to the Hawkins, Domingo, and Bowles Families. This play is dedicated to 5212 Chancellor Street in West Philadelphia. This play is dedicated to Soul Music. Thank you Mom, Pop, Averie, Rick, Phillip, Raul Aktanov, Maurice McRae, Anika, Noni Rose, Lisa Ramirez, Lisa Kron,

15

Leigh Fondakowski, Ariel, Shafir, Barbie Stein, Queva Lutz, Margo Hall, Tony Kelly, Hillary Cohen, Jessica Levine, Zach Willis, Robert Driggs, Marc Ohrem LeClef, Stacey Robinson, Crystal Durant, Charlie, Schroder, Milissa Carey, Jim Nicola, Linda Chapman, Lisa Peterson, Edie Robb and Stevie Smith at Station Three Management, Teresa Wolf and Josh Schiowitz at the Schiowitz, Conner, Ankrum and Wolf Agency, Joe's Pub/ Public Theater, Kate Navin and the Abrams Artists Agency, Lauren Tobin at Panther PR. Doug Aibel and the entire staff of The Vineyard Theater.

ABOUT THE CREATOR

Colman Domingo is the author of *Wild with Happy*, *A Boy and his Soul*, *Up Jumped Springtime*, and *The Brothers*. The artistic work of Mr. Domingo has been honored with a Tony, Drama Desk and Drama League nomination. His work has won an OBIE, Lucille Lortel, GLAAD, Connecticut Critics Circle, Bay Area Theater Critics Circle and Internet Theater Bloggers Award. Colman has received fellowships and/or residencies from The Sundance Theater Lab, The People's Light and Theater Company, and the Banff Playwrights Colony. Mr. Domingo is currently under commission from The American Conservatory Theater. His plays have been produced at The Public Theater, The Vineyard Theater, Theatreworks, Philadelphia Theater Company, Baltimore Centerstage, Tricycle Theatre (London), Theater Rhinoceros and Thick Description Theater. Mr. Domingo as an actor has starred on Broadway in *Passing Strange, Chicago, Well* and *The Scottsboro Boys* and has worked in films such as Lee Daniel's *The Butler, Lincoln, Red Hook Summer, Passing Strange, Miracle at St. Ana, King of the Bingo Game* and *Newlyweeds* among others.

For Edie, Clarence, Rick, Averie and Phillip.

Characters

All characters are played by one man with just a simple gesture. There is something about the magic of one person transforming without the use of clothing changes etc. Just voice, body, and a gesture to become our storyteller, his younger self, mother, stepfather, sister, brother, aunts and uncles etc. There is even a crack ho stripper that is a lot of fun to play just by shifting the body and voice.

Setting:
A theatrical space and a basement of infinite possibilities!

Stuff:
A stereo circa early 1970's, many crates with soul music LPs
and 45s. An artificial white Christmas tree, ten speed bikes,
toys, an E-Z Bake oven, string lights, black Sheba poster,
barstools, boxes etc. Things that populate the memory of an
inner city black home that frames the story.

Place:
In a theatrical space. The archives of our memory.

Time:
Today, Yesterday and Tomorrow.

Author's Note:
This play SHOULD NOT be read without the required music
if possible. The music is a major component to the piece. The
piece is also very physical and it moves at a quick pace of
about 85 minutes with no intermission. Have fun. Read this
play with a glass of scotch and wearing your favorite Kaftan.

Enjoy.

Seriously tho. A Kaftan.

Music Playlist

1. "THE SOUND OF PHILADELPHIA (TSOP)"
   Songwriters/Composers: Kenneth Gamble and Leon Huff
   Performed by: The Three Degrees
   Publishers/Administrators:
   1. Sony/ATV Songs LLC
   2. Warner-Tamerlane Publishing Corporation

2. "THERE'LL NEVER BE"
   Written by: Robert De Barge
   Performed by: Switch
   Publisher/Administrator: Jobete Music Corporation Incorporated,
   EMI Music Publishing

3. "LIVING FOR THE LOVE OF YOU"
   Songwriters/Composers: Charles Alvin Beasley Jr., Don Thigpen
   Performed by: Isley Brothers
   Publishers/Administrators: Big Brother Jonathan Publishing Company

4. "IT'S A MAN'S MAN'S MAN'S WORLD"
   Songwriters/Composers: James Brown and Betty Jean Newsome
   Performed by: James Brown
   Publishers/Administrators:
   1. Dynatone Publishing Company
   2. Warner-Tamerlane Publishing Corporation

5. "SHINING STAR"
   Written by: Philip James Bailey, Lorenzo Russell Dunn, Maurice White
   Performed by: Earth, Wind and Fire
   Publishers/Administrators: EMI April Music Incorporated, c/o EMI
   Music Publishing

6. "DAYDREAMING"
   Songwriter/Composer: Aretha Franklin
   Performed by: Aretha Franklin
   Publishers/Administrators: Springtime Music Incorporated

7. "SWEET STICKY THING"
   Songwriters/Composers: Willie Beck, Leroy Bonner, Marshall Eugene
   Jones, Ralph Middlebrooks, Marvin R. Pierce, Clarence Satchell,
   James Rodger Williams
   Performed by: The Ohio Players
   Publishers/Administrators:
   1. Rick's Music Incorporated
   2. Segundo Suenos LLC

8. "YOU CAN'T HIDE FROM YOURSELF"
   Songwriter/Composer: Kenneth Gamble, Leon Huff
   Performed by: Teddy Pendergrass
   Publisher: Warner-Tamerlane Publishing Corporation

9. "HUSTLE"
   Songwriter/Composer: Van McCoy
   Performed by: Van McCoy
   Publishers/Administrator:
   1. Van McCoy Music Incorporated
   2. Warner-Tamerlane Publishing Corporation

10 "BETWEEN THE SHEETS"
   Written by: Ernest Isley, Marvin Isley, O'Kelly Isley, Ronald Isley,
   Rudolph Bernard Isley and Christopher H. Jasper
   Performed by: Isley Brothers
   Publisher/Administrator:
   1. Bovina Music Incorporated, c/o EMI April Music Incorporated,
   c/o EMI Music Publishing
   2. EMI April Music Incorporated, c/o EMI Music Publishing

11 "BAD GIRLS"
   Songwriters/Composers: Joseph Patrick Esposito, Edward Peter
   Hokenson, Bruce Sudano, Donna Summer
   Performed by: Donna Summer
   Publishers/Administrators:
   1. Earborne Music
   2. Rick's Music Incorporated

12 "I'M COMING OUT"
   Songwriters/Composers: Bernard Edwards and Nile Gregory Rodgers
   Performed by: Diana Ross
   Publishers/Administrators:
   1. Bernard's Other Music
   2. Song/ATV Songs LLC

13 "BETCHA BY GOLLY WOW"
   Songwriters/Composers: Thomas Randolph Bell and Linda Epstein
   Performed by: The Stylistics
   Publisher/Administrator: Warner-Tamerlane Publishing Corporation

14 "DO DO WAP IS STRONG IN HERE"
   Songwriter/Composer: Curtis Mayfield
   Performed by: Curtis Mayfield
   Publishers/Administrator:
   1. Mayfield Music
   2. Todd Mayfield Publishing

15 "FIRE"
   Songwriter/Composer: James Williams, Clarence Satchell, Leroy
   Bonner,Marshall Jones, Ralph Middlebrooks, Marvin Pierce, William
   Beck
   Performed by: The Ohio Players
   Publisher: Mercury Records

16 YOU CAN'T HIDE FROM YOURSELF"
   Songwriter/Composer: Kenneth Gamble, Leon Huff
   Performed by: Teddy Pendergrass
   Publisher: Warner-Tamerlane Publishing Corporation

17 "CRUSIN"
   Written by: William Robinson and Marvin Tarplin
   Performed by: Smokey Robinson
   Publisher/Administrator: Music Company, c/o EMI April Music
   Incorporated, c/o EMI Music Publishing

18 "YOU'RE THE BEST THING THAT EVER HAPPENED TO ME"
   Written by: James Dexter Weatherly
   Performed by: Gladys Knight and The Pips
   Publisher/Administrator: Universal Polygram International Publishing
   Incorporated

19 "FAMILY REUNION"
    Written by: Kenny Gamble and Leon Huff
    Performed by: The O'Jay's
    Publisher/Administrator: Warner-Tamerlane Publishing Corporation

20 "SHOW YOU THE WAY TO GO"
    Written by: Kenny Gamble and Leon Huff
    Performed by: The Jackson's
    Publisher/Administrator: Warner-Tamerlane Publishing Corporation

21 "SOMEDAY WE'LL ALL BE FREE"
    Written by: Donny Hathaway and Edward Howard
    Performed by: Donny Hathaway
    Publishers/Administrators:
    1. Kuumba c/o Universal Music – MGB Songs
    2. Universal Music – MGB Songs
    3. W B Music Corporation, Warner Chappell Music Incorporated

22 "CAN YOU FEEL IT"
    Written by: Michael and Jackie Jackson
    Performed by: The Jacksons
    Publisher/Administrator: Epic

JAY sits on the corner of the stage thumbing through a heap of albums. Lots of Vinyl. Stevie Wonder's "As" plays… then JAY takes the needle off of the record.

JAY: My parents were selling the house that I grew up in. 5212 Chancellor Street in West Philadelphia. The house that Mom bought for 15,000 dollars and made it our "bump and hustle" palace! The neighborhood that gave birth to Will Smith, Patti LaBelle, Wilt Chamberlain and Guy Blueford the first black astronaut! I was entering my mid thirties as a struggling artist in New York and struggling to stay on top of my parents affairs as they dealt with finances and aging. My parents were selling the only home that I ever knew and that was wearing me out!

My parents made the move "down south" after West Philly made its economic transition from loving educated working-class families to drug and thug central. Sad but one of the many black neighborhoods ravaged by Reaganomics to continue slavery under the guise of "ghetto!" But I digress.

My mom asked me to go to Philly to give the house a cleaning before the real estate broker went by. Years of neglect from renting the house out to a single mother with like two hundred kids, the house looked like a hot buttered mess! Water damage, mold, and paint chipped ceilings. Morning glories weren't blooming in the backyard. The hardwood floors my stepfather sanded and refinished looked dull and tired. Ya'll, my childhood home looked like a WORN OUT HO after fleet week!

I cleaned from the top floor to the basement. The basement was filled with all the left behind remnants of yesteryear: A filthy white artificial Christmas tree, the rusty E Z bake oven that my brother Rick made efficient use of by cooking my sister Averie's doll heads in. A rotary phone with a cord that was stretched out for at least nine feet! My precious violin that had my nickname J.J., short for my middle name, Jason, engraved on the back. A cracked disco ball that was spinning at every famous, Clarence and Edie, New Year's Eve "throwdown's!" A stereo with an eight track player! In the far corner of the basement, stacks of dusty old crates. Left behind in the movin' on up of the 1990s was the music that made our house a happy home. Filled with Soul!

(He puts a record on the stereo. It is "The Sound of Philadelphia".)

This is the sound of a soul. Philly, New York, San Francisco and everywhere in-between! The sound of a backyard barbecue in the

ghetto, the slick juicy sound of Don Cornelius,
my nappy hair being picked out for Sunday
school and watchful childhood eyes.

My Soul Music is my sanctuary, y'all…Soul
Music is my life.

(He turns up the music…magically.)

This is the sound of my "Young America".
Double-Dutch and Penny Candy, Hot and
Cold Butter Beans Come and Get your
Supper! Corn Rows and Braids! Afros and
Jheri Curls! Slow Drags and House Parties!
Bass lines on a Rufus track! The roar of my
Pop's Pontiac Riviera and my brother Rick's
Kangol hat! This is the sound of my sister
Averie's ghetto girl strut!

(He enjoys the music.)

This is the sound of my heart, my feet, my
eyes. The train as it moves up and down
the east coast from dreams and the state
of confusion to family and the state of
confession. The quest to find beauty in this
crazy ass world! The sound of my Mother's
love, the bass in my Pop's throat, the sound
of my loved one's hands soothing the beast
within, the sound of the weight that I will take
the load that is to be carried! The heavens
have sent angels with golden throats and

Cadillacs. *Diamond in the back, sunroof top diggin' the scene with a gangster lean, Oooh Oooh!!!*

This is the sound of RE RUN and SHIRLEY! GOOD TIMES and fine ass THELMA! SYLVESTER and DIANA! COOLEY HIGH and UPTOWN SATURDAY NIGHT!

(He dances.)

I'm dancing for the sound that dances within me. In the name of the God Father, I thank you, I am your son, and I've got the Holy Ghost. I've got to give it up. I've got to…I've got to…I've got to get it on.

(Music fades out.)

Now that is the *Sound of Philadelphia.* M.other F.ather S.ister B.rother.

(The SWITCH song "THERE'LL NEVER BE A BETTER LOVE" pumps in.)

Philly Soul was the major player but the likes of Detroit, LA, and the other soul havens made their "Impressions!" Look at all this! Ahhh! … *(He flips through the albums.)*

Stevie Wonder
Marvin Gaye
Curtis Mayfield

Donny Hathaway

The Silvers with those big ass afros!
The Spinners
The Temptations
The Commodores
Harold Melvin and the Blue Notes
Gladys Night and the Pips...
LTD, Love Tenderness and Devotion...damn,
Can I get a Witness?
Luther Vandross
Barry White
Phyllis Hyman
Rufus Featuring Chaka Khan, Chaka Khan!

And Switch!

There'll never be a better love.

(To an audience member.)

Are you even down with switch? Do you even
know who switch is?

Let me tell you, there will never be a better
love.

*(He sings the proper opening lyrics of the song after
the spoken word intro.)*

There will never be a better love! Whooo!!!
We listened to so much music in that house.

How could they leave this music behind? A
lot of the albums were warped and damaged
but they still had glory on their grooves. That
day in the basement the vinyl just hung in the
air like ghosts. Dancing and cooing! Those
ghosts were always there to shed some light in
the darkness, put a smile on your face or put
you in a sexy ass mood or to delve just a little
deeper – to keep it real. You can't help it, just
from the intro you're hooked –

*(The ISLEY BROTHERS. "LIVING FOR THE
LOVE OF YOU".)*

Awww shit. I just have to marinate on this
for a minute. After almost burning down the
backyard during a family barbecue, my uncle
Jerome would be like,

UNCLE JEROME: Aw Yeah! That's my song!
Turn that up! Mmph! Hallelujah! *Driftin' on a
memory…*

JAY: Do you know this song? Do you? My family
was all about this music. I was born into
SOUL MUSIC. My Mom, Edie, came from
a large and faithful family where not one but
both of her parents were pastors of Baptist
churches. The only time you heard secular
music in my grandparent's house was at big
family gatherings where the visiting reverend,
James Brown, took his cue. In my parent's

house, that is, my mom and stepfather's, Soul Music was the Gospel. 2-4-7. *(Sings.) Glad to be...here along with a lover unlike no other.* My mom didn't forget about spirituals on Sunday afternoons or a little Leontyne Price on Sunday evenings just to give us little chir'en a little culture *(Leontyne Price singing Visi D'arte or something of the like creeps in.)*, although Leontyne would sing out for about 15 seconds before my stepfather Clarence would put his foot down and change the music to something that he believed was a bit blacker. *(Leontyne cuts out – "Living for the Love of You" resumes).*

Soul Music takes me to barbecues, block parties, family reunions, and car trips down south, where my mom packed deviled eggs sprinkled with paprika on top and fried chicken! Fried hard with lard! Soul Music takes me to those lazy summer nights taping your favorites off the radio after calling them in with a dedication to the girl you want to "go" with. *(Mock young lover voice.)* "Do I stand a Chance?"

Remember listening to 8 tracks and 45s? And cursing that someone broke the last yellow disc that goes in the middle so that you could play your jam on the component set. I used to love to watch the records drop one after the other.

In my family and many families like my own, Soul Music was a relative, that was loud as hell, always doing the "four corners" and always getting you up on your feet. It took me a while though. I was a rebel. I rebelled against Soul Music in my early years. I wanted to be like the high-class people like on *Dynasty*. You never saw Blake and Crystal Carrington doing the "tootsie roll" to a nasty Millie Jackson song. I was such a nerd growing up in the inner sanctums of West Philadelphia in the late 70s early 80s. Glasses, buck teeth, pimply skin, awful posture and a beloved relationship with the public library where I was free from the confines of inner city life to immerse myself in the Ancient Pyramids at Giza, or listen to the really sweet light-skinned librarian with the mushroom hairdo, read to me the latest Encyclopedia Brown mystery. My favorite. And when I wasn't in the library, I was practising my precious violin, diligently, on the enclosed porch after school. My pop made the porch my rehearsal hall.

POP: Boy! If you ain't gonna play something that I can sing along with and do the sho nuff sho nuff, put it out there on that enclosed porch. I just need to eat my chicken in peace. I work too damn hard. Breaking my back and not taking no shit. I just need some quiet! Chicken and Quiet!

JAY: Mom encouraged my love of things that
    were not of the inner city ilk. I would always
    hear my mom coming to my defense when
    I started taking clarinet, violin, and ballet
    lessons...

EDIE: Oh Clarence, just because Jay Jay wants
    to try something "different", don't mean
    he's going to turn out to be funny acting like
    cousin SIFERDEAN!

JAY: Siferdean was the cousin that you rarely
    heard of...because he was "funny". I
    asked my mom one day how do you spell
    SIFERDEAN! She quickly snapped –

EDIE: IT CAN'T BE SPELLED!

JAY: My pop would take one look at me doing
    my pliés, relevés, bate mats and shake his
    head

POP: Mmph mmmp mmppp...

JAY: He'd go to the stereo and turn on some
    James Brown, usually, the song,

    (Music cue: James Brown's "A Man's World".)

    I'd pick up the Violin in sharp defiance and
    practise my Beethoven as fast as my tiny
    hands could.

(Music fades out.)

JAY: All of that changed the day that it was my sister Averie's turn to baby-sit me. It was the end of the summer of 1978 and I was nine years old and my sister had free concert tickets for summer stage at the Mann Music Center in Fairmount Park. The headliner was EARTH, WIND AND FIRE!

Well, to me, a classically trained violinist – I thought it would be a big YAWN!!! So I sat smoking my Newport cigarette, that I blackmailed my fifteen-year-old big sister into giving me or

9-YEAR-OLD JAY: I'mma tell Mommy you smokin' if you don't give me one!

JAY: You see I was a nerd but I had an inner-city bad boy deep within! I looked at all of the pretty black faces in the crowd. Some woman with an Afro bigger than Angela Davis' looked at me with disapproval as if to say,

ANGELA DAVIS AFRO ROCKIN' WOMAN: That's a damn shame… Smokin'!!! That effeminate little peazy headed nigga needs his ass whipped with an ironing cord!

JAY: I knew that look well…that was the same typical matriarchal look that Momma from that television show *What's Happening* used to chastise Rog and Dee with. Naturally I put the cigarette out.

9-YEAR-OLD JAY: The lights went out. All you could hear was the sound of black folks screaming with ecstasy. Out of the vast darkness all you could see was the glimmer of what would later be revealed as costumes and the glow of black oiled skin. Then I heard a rumble. No, not a rumble, an earthquake!!! And then the tinkling sounds of chimes. And then, the whooshing gusts of wind. A baritone voice made its way through the darkness. Reverb made the isolated voice haunting and delirious. "The Elements of the World… EARTH…WIND –", and when he said WIND, the melee of the audience began to whip themselves into frenzy as if Jesus Christ and the Apostles were about to appear on that stage! I searched the darkness for a string section that I could focus on. Something that I could relate to!

(Music cue: Earth Wind And Fire "Shining Star".)

JAY: Then the voice finally said, right at the moment when the crowd couldn't take any more, "FIRE!" Goddamn! Explosions from everywhere! Fireworks rained down on the stage like stars! I was sure I was going blind! Out of that incandescent, transplendence at least twenty men were revealed in shimmering skintight drag! All you could see was lights, glitter, and crotch! I thought that I had died and gone to heaven. I'm just kidding! I was only nine years old! But I couldn't hide from the fate that Soul Music was about to deliver. I couldn't hide from my (a la Soul Train) SOOOUUUUUL!

(Dance break filled with the "robot", "electric boogie", "popping and locking", and finally "the Prince love sexy" then to stillness.)

EDIE: Jay Jay cut that down! Cut that down son! They gonna call the cops round here!

Come on honey it's a hot one tonight. *(She wipes her brow and gets her bottle of water, she notices the moon, it's breathtaking.)* Come sit down here with your momma. And bring me that transistor!

JAY: In the backyard of that house, when I was young, Mom and I would chill out on balmy eastern nights listening to the quiet storm on WDAS FM that started at around 11pm. In the summer I could stay up as long as I wanted to, and my mother's company was the best. We would sit and she would tell me stories of when she was my age. She was the youngest of eleven children in a very poor family.

When she was my age, she would play with her cut-out paper dolls and she and her cut-outs would speak French as she imagined *(mock French)* and she and her cut-outs would travel to foreign lands. Foreign from the inner city of Philadelphia like, Pensacola, Florida!

JAY: She would tell me tales of my biological dad and how she was enamored of his Central American heritage even though he was a

EDIE: No-good low-life low-life "Spick" who robbed me of my youth!

JAY: This was before my big strong blue collar of a stepfather Clarence came along to be my pop and took over where Dad took off. In the backyard Mom spoke of many places that she wanted me to see and things she wanted me to do...

EDIE: Like go to art museums, play instruments, and I want you to go the the-ater like the white folks and see operas and things, travel the world baby, go far away from this neighborhood, but don't forget where you come from! And in your travels, don't forget to pick me up a kaftan with the dolman sleeves just like the one Diana Ross wears in your favorite movie, *Mahogany*! You are so very intelligent; you're my special boy. *(She blots the sweat from under her boobs.)* Keep a song in your heart and you will always find your way.

JAY: One starry night as we sat sipping Lipton Iced Tea out of tall, colored aluminum tumblers, Mommy asked me to run in the house and grab her pocketbook because the new moon was emblazoned in the sky. The new moon as Mom said promised

EDIE: New Money, New Experiences and New Dreams!

JAY: Peering out behind the Locust Movie Theater sign on the corner of the block the New Moon was shining, titillating and taunting the inner-city muted night, beckoning Newness. I made a quick dash to grab Mom's pocketbook. That was positioned with care on the end table in the living room next to the L-shaped white sofa with the plastic covering. Running, brimming with excitement, almost tripping over Mom's hot pink Doctor Scholls clogs left on the plastic runner that led to the back door. I handed her her rust-colored pocketbook with the peppermint and butterscotch candy whispering at the bottom! With the look of diamonds and caviar in her eyes and a smile on her lips, my mom threw open the pleather five and dime handbag. A ritual – to fill it with blessings. The Sultry Voice on the radio sent out a special request.

RADIO ANNOUNCER: This goes out to Wakim
   Abdul Shafir in South West Philly with love
   from his foxy lady, Stacey from Mount Airy.
   Keep it right here all night, on the quiet storm
   WDAS FM.

(Music cue: Aretha Franklin "Daydreaming".)

EDIE: Jay Jay... Listen.

JAY: My mother gazed longingly at the New
   Moon. I gazed in silence too. No words just
   eyes calling on the moon. And the sound of
   the background singers setting the tone. In
   an instant, with just the sound of a song, I
   saw my mother's thoughts leave the modest
   backyard of the low-income row home. With
   just the sound of a song, I saw my mother
   leave her hard religious and stifling childhood,
   a string of bad relationships and broken
   promises. I saw a broken but hopeful woman
   with her hair tied up in an Afrocentric wrap,
   leave her disappointment of abandoning an
   Ivy League University, the first in her family
   to go to college, she, a bronze-coloured
   nineteen-year-old in love with a strange
   and beautiful man from Belize and knocked
   up! With just the sound of that song, I saw
   my mother leave poverty, and worry, and
   sadness, and hopelessness of being a black
   woman on welfare in 1978 with three children
   who makes a little money cleaning houses,

coming home with bags of leftovers: Matzah, Gifelta Fish, Stale Bagels and Lox. I loved the Rugelach for dessert! Tonight, Mom was regal in the light of the new moon as Aretha daydreamed at night in our ears with the promise of –

EDIE: New Money, New Experiences, and New Dreams.

JAY: I told my mom that I wanted New Money, New Experiences and New Dreams, but how am I supposed to get them if I don't have a pocketbook? She just looked at me this little skinny child of nine and said,

EDIE: Turn that up for me son. *(Aretha swells.)*

O Sweetheart…just hold open your hands! Let god see that you are open for change. Right Ree Ree! *(Meaning Aretha.)*

(CLARENCE sings the first two lines of the chorus.)

JAY: On a humid eastern night sat a boy and his mommy. Listening to Aretha and holding small hands and a pocketbook, waiting… Sometimes in the summer when the sky is clear, and the moon is new, I turn on some Aretha and hold these hands wide open. Lord knows my heart, my soul, the federal government, and the woman who still calls me every so often from the student loan repayment center, still craves New Money, New Experiences and New Dreams for me! Whenever I hear that song I can still hear my mom saying,

EDIE: Just because you wish for it don't mean it won't come true. Just Believe. Hold tight and hold open your hands!

(Music cue: Ohio Players "Sweet Sticky Thing".)

JAY: Back in the basement I dusted off the Ohio Players album with the hot chocolate mama with gold bracelets and slicked-backed hair on the cover! Damn, these women were fine as hell. And the Ohio Players knew women and how to celebrate them. "You Sweet Sticky Thing"…

(He sings a phrase of the opening lyrics.)

JAY: I don't know about you but when I was a kid I had no idea what "You sweet sticky thing" was all about. Now I know. Kinda!

(Music fades out.)

The things you see with adult eyes. You know like, Thrift Shops. I hated going to Thrift Shops when I was a kid. Up until I was 16 and able to get a part-time job at McDonald's to pick up some cash of my own, I was always subjected to the ravages of this place called

"The Second Time Around!" And, no, it wasn't named after the popular Shalimar song, it was the name of the second-hand clothing, furniture, shoe, glassware, toy, hobby and artificial plant store that was my mother's form of crack. We were in that emporium for hours at a time. My mother always said, "They are just like new". I thought, if they were just like new, then I want new. I despised the mothball and stale smell of what I perceived as "used". Now, thankfully, in these "Money's too tight to Mention" *(Ad-lib about the economic downturn in some topical way.)*, I know the value of them and you can't keep me out of the muthafuckas!

The things you see with Adult Eyes. Like, Tom Jones. I had no idea what Mom's fascination was with Tom Jones every Friday night on CBS. She and my aunts never missed an episode. My Aunt Thelma would tell me –

AUNT THELMA: *(In a cigarette-riddled voice.)* Now go on over to Punchie's Deli and check to see if my number hit! And pick me up a pack of Pell Mell's and get yourself some Now Laters or Pop Rocks with the change. Let us ladies alone with Mr. Tom Jones for about an hour. Edie! Come on! It's on! It's on!

JAY: It was not until I caught a few reruns on VH1 that I realized their fascination. That

man had the biggest bulge in his pants that
1978 would allow. Extraordinary! With adult
eyes I can actually hear more clearly. These
old LPs and 45s… Now, I understand, they
were flipping out some serious shit about
life that are timeless. Brothers and Sisters
like Marvin, Donny, Aretha and Curtis were
singing about some important stuff. Human
Kindness, The Ecology, War, Politics and
Love. Fuckin too! But Love! Good Old-
Fashioned Love.

My stepfather Clarence is what I would call
a con-negro-seur of Soul Music. A few years
back, over a two-piece and a biscuit, he told
me

POP. Yeah Son, they don't make good Soul
Music no mo! To get into soul you've gots
to go deep. Unearth the good, the bad, the
ugly, the beautiful. Plain and simple – truth!
LADY GAGA AIN'T GONNA GIVE IT TO
YOU! Neither will, what's her name Edie?
RIHANNA! Now, USHER, he's trying to
come with it but he's got some living to do.
Now, Mary J. Blige, De'Angelo, Adele-whoo-I
like that thick English girl, big thighs, Lauren
Hill, even tho she done lost her damned
mind, Jill Scott-you know she from Philly too
– they are direct arteries to the roots of soul
these days.

I can't get into no – what was that song called Edie? "My milkshake brings all the boys to the yard!" "Move bitch get out the way!" "To the window to the wall til the sweat drippin' from big balls!!!" That ain't no music! *(He gets up with a strain.)* Oh Lawd! Give me some, "Come on get up get down get funky loose" or some "Turn off the lights and light a candle." Give me some soul that churns the chicken grease in your heart!

(Music cue: Teddy Pendergrass "You Can't Hide From Yourself".)

Oh Lawd. Listen to that bass line. *(Turns music down.)* Car accident and transsexuals, I don't give a damn, Teddy Pendergass is and will always be a "Soul Music God." *(Turns music up and sings along – badly.)*

(Turns music down.) And Michael Jackson. A Soul Music God! Black, white or alien they broke the mold when they made that boy! *(He sits)* Michael Jackson. A Soul Music God! I don't know what that boy did behind closed doors with kids, women, bubbles the monkey or the elephant man's bones, his creativity and contribution to the world is much larger than his fucked-up-ed-ness! You gotsa take the bad with the good. After all he was only a man! Trying to hide a lot of pain. Wearing masks and glittery gloves. But you can't hide

from yourself. Right Teddy? You can't hide from the soul. *(Turns music up.)*

You can't hide from yourself…
Anywhere you go, there you are

Remember son; there is always a message in the music.

(CLARENCE riffs with TEDDY for a bit. He then, transitions back to JAY.)

JAY: How could my parents leave this music behind? Did the world change that much? It had to be an accident. Listen to the way that these people express themselves in this music. With so much passion and spirit. They left behind, Oh My God, Aunt Thelma's Dee Dee Sharp Gamble, Pop's Peaches and Herb, Mom's Spinners, Rick's George Benson, Averie's Evelyn "Champagne" King, and my… *(Music cuts out abruptly.)* Carpenters!

Musical tastes vary! *(He puts the album back into the crate.)* My sister Averie told me one day over some loud music while chain-smoking a pack of Newports that…

AVERIE: I'm a Nigga! I don't put on no airs for nobody, I like my music loud and my men tough as HELL. If somebody don't want to hear my music, buy some earplugs or move the fuck off the block! What!?

JAY: Averie, a delicate flower, actually introduced
me to the sounds of Donna Summer,
Sylvester, and the Silvers. Disco! *(Music cue:
"The Hustle".)* When we were growing up
her best friends were Donny and Martin.
Donny loved wearing eyeliner and lip-
gloss. Martin was very bowlegged and was
amazing at Double Dutch, even though boys
weren't supposed to play. With adult eyes and
information I realize that my tough-ass big
sister was a huge fag hag! I remember the day
that Averie and her boys came in the house
filled with excitement about this new dance,
this new dance called… *(Sound blasts! "Do
the Hustle!" He dances.)* I watched Averie and
Martin's bell-bottoms swing gracefully as they
twirled, rollicking with glee. My brother Rick
would come home from Karate practice and –

RICK: Cut his eyes at Averie and the two
twirling Disco globes of manhood and go
to his bedroom and blast his cassette player.
(Mouths.) Faggot!

(Music cue: Rick James "Cold Blooded".)

JAY: Every so often in my parents' house, there
was virtually a battle of sounds! Especially on
a Saturday night!

AVERIE: Cut that down Rick, we are trying to
dance!

RICK: Trying is the operative word!

AVERIE: Spell operative?

RICK: That's why you ain't got no titties!

AVERIE: Nigga!

RICK: I'MMA TELL MOM YOU CALLED ME
A NIGGA! NIGGA THIS, NO TITTIES!
(He blasts the Rick James.)

9-YEAR-OLD JAY: Ooooh! I'mma tell Mom ya'll
calling each other niggers!

AVERIE: Shut up punk! She ain't home. Her or
Pop! I'm running thangs now! *(All music cuts
abruptly.)* It's SATURDAY NIGHT!

JAY: Saturday night! Saturday night was the Battle
Royal of Soul Music in my house. My brother
Rick would be in his bedroom primping for
his pimping to the sound of the Isley's. *(Music
cue: Isley's "Between the Sheets".)*

His costume for the night and his step show-
would consist of a white IZOD shirt, white
pleated gabardine pants and white shell
top Adidas. A fat ass gold chain around his
neck! A white Kangol hat. He'd slap on
some Drakkar Noir and top it all off with his
Gazelle sunglasses on that mug of impeccable

masculinity and stand in the mirror and
POSE!!! *(Music up.)*

AVERIE: Cut that down, Rick, cut that down; I'm
trying to get dressed!

RICK: Shut up itty-bitty-titty committee!

AVERIE: Shut up you Black Dog!

RICK: Heifer!!!

AVERIE: Dookey breath!

RICK: BALD-HEADED WEASEL!

AVERIE: BLACKETY, BLACK, BLACK,
BLACK!!!

13-YEAR-OLD JAY: Ave and Rick could you cut
your music down; I can't concentrate on my
Beethoven.

JAY: Averie

AVERIE: *(Lip pop sound.)* Trying to drown out
that sexy, smooth R and B and Classical la
la la! would jam her component set up to the
highest meter.

(Music cue: Bad Girls.)

(She does the Lucy Booty Dance – nastily.)

JAY: With adult eyes and ears, I am not quite
sure whether my sister was a tomboy or a fag
herself. She'd prance in front of her mirror.
Her trademark attire was fashioned to hang
out with her "boys" at the newest, greatest
invention, "The Mall!" Gloria Vanderbilt ass-
threatening jeans, a lime green tube top high
top pink Pro-Keds – and she'd part and grease
her well permed isometric haircut – that had
a shelf in the back, and then she'd POSE.
(Music up.) When she'd catch me peeking in
the keyhole she would lip-synch over to my
view and then turn her butt to the door *(Music
out.)* and fart. Somehow she could do it on
command.

I was in my bedroom with the usual 13-year-
old complaint. LOVE. Every teenager wants
to be wanted. Wants the girlfriend. Especially
if you are a little soft like me because it's
important for your masculinity! It's important
to your family. It's part of being a strong black
man. Rick knew how to talk to girls, All of the
guys in the songs knew how to talk to girls. I
was still trying. I would give it my best shot.
I would put on my favorite purple paisley
polyester print pullover and I would put on
my favorite song and POSE!!! *(Music cue:
Diana Ross "I'm Coming Out".)*

Somehow I didn't think that would be the way to pick up girls. But it sure made me feel real good.

Now, after my brother and sister made curfew and I was tucked in bed watching a late-night Linda Blair movie, my parents would come in from socializing.

(Music cue: The Stylistics "Betcha By Golly Wow".)

Me and my sister and brother would always sneak to the top of the stairs and my parents would come in from tearing up the town, you know, they had a little Thunderbird on their breath! And my pop would be like "Come here woman, Come on girl" and my mom's like "Oh no, no get out of here, the kids, the kids sleep – Shhhhh, lawd have mercy, horny ass man!!!" But he would just ignore her, chase her around the room – you know, a little cat and mouse. Finally catch up with her, grab her by the hips, and he would be all "Come here Edie." – *(He dances.)* Shhhhh… Yeahhhh!!!

(Sings.)

There's a spark of magic in your eyes…

And he would sing to her. Rick, Ave and I would giggle and shhh each other.

This is my music! Maybe it's because my pop would just sing to my mom! We were witnesses to "Black Love!" Love that you saw advertised by K Tel. Love that lasts! You know, when you can sing to the one that you love with an open heart. Even with a little liquor on your breath. That love just may last. I think so because I have witnessed it and I saw that whenever things got tense, or the road got hard it was just…

(CLARENCE sings the chorus and then the next verse and then the chorus all the while interjecting with "Do you know this song?", "Sing with me if you want to", and "This is your one time!" and "One more time." before the last chorus. During this song JAY becomes the Stylistics and the whole mood is that of the period.)

(Music fades under during this monologue.)

JAY: My parents' love was in the music. I could feel it. My love would be in the music too! I always knew that it wouldn't look like Edie and Clarence. More like Clarence and Clarence! O.K., no, that vision is too alarming. But you know what I mean! I <u>was</u> my mother's special boy, my pop's mmmp, mmmp, mmmp. And Rick and Averie's little brother who admired Kangol hats and the hustle and the music. *(He goes over to the albums and pulls out Marvin Gaye's "Let's Get It On."*

JAY reads the liner notes on the back of the album and emulates Marvin Gaye.)

"I can't see anything wrong with sex between two consenting anybodies. I think we make far too much of it. After all one's genitals are just one important part of the magnificent human body. I contend that SEX IS SEX and LOVE IS LOVE. When combined they work well together. But they are really two discrete needs and should be treated as such. Have your sex. It can be very exciting if you are lucky. I hope the music I present here makes you lucky."

In that house at 13, I was a student at the University of Marvin Gaye, The Stylistics, and The Delfonics. At 15, Stacey Lattisaw, Michael Jackson, and Jeffery Osbourne. At 17, Prince, Atlantic Star, Klymaxx, and Ready for the World.

By the time I was a freshman in college I had a few friends that wanted to take me to a club to "experience" some new music. When I was in college, my two very curious friends, who shall remain nameless, Guy Talley and Robert Luis Driggs. They dragged me to this hole in the wall black gay bar called A2's. It was so scary. The men there were either these old white zinfandel-sipping queens or these hard-ass looking boys. The trip for me was that there were people there that didn't look like what I thought was gay, you know what I mean, they look like thugs and shit. But some of them would open their mouths and they're like, "Hi you doin?"

They look like they're going to take your last food stamp, but then they open their mouths and a string of pearls and a purse falls out! Blew my mind.

So check this shit out. *(Music cue: "Do Do Wap is Strong in Here".)* We started going there all the time and we went there once and they announced that it was Miss Roxie's Birthday. <u>Miss Roxie's Birthday!!!</u> It was cute for a minute. They had this stripper dancing to that song. "You can take a piece of my love." Anyway the stripper starts dancing around with this huge monstrous piece of flesh and there was a crowd surrounding Miss Roxie, the overweight glamorous drag queen. Baby, the stripper starts slapping Ms. Roxie in the face with that baby's arm and then I noticed that Miss Roxie...

(Music cuts out abruptly.)...was my cousin Siferdean.

My infamous cousin Siferdean that no one dare spoke a word of. I believe that it was at someone's funeral reception that Siferdean was exposed. His "job" at this funeral reception was to show people where the bathroom was. Well, with some of the men he took a long time with. All these men kept going upstairs and my Aunt Thelma was wondering *(Aunt Thelma.)* "what was taking them so long?"

Well, Siferdean was charging five dollars for a blowjob. Now I know that some of you, with adult eyes, may think that that is very reasonable!

Listen. I was still very much in the closet and if Siferdean saw me in that club, seeing him, getting a piece of his love, it would have been over. I was on the run! From Siferdean! From myself!

Until one night it all caught up with me at "Poochie's Brown Biscuits." You don't know Poochie's? That was my brother Rick's "spot." *(Music cue: "Fire")* and he wanted to take me there for a lap dance for my 21st birthday. Immediately Rick has some girl, as he would say, "Popping her coochie and shoving her tig ole bitties in his face."

JAY: Amused and feeling like a big-ass fraud, I'm like, "Rick why don't we go somewhere else quieter so we can catch up" and he's like...

RICK: Naw, you gotta wait for Aquafonesha to come out, she's really "live!"

JAY: One of these girl marches straight over to me. She looked like a straight up crack ho, just within arm's reach of the pipe. She was sucking on what appeared to be a dill pickle and was not opposed to making radical gestures with her tongue and the vegetable.

(The CRACK HO STRIPPER backs her thang up.)

CRACK HO STRIPPER: Hey there slim jim, would you like to watch me make my love come down?

JAY: I guess…

Well she starts her gyration of "ass on lap" *(Music up.)*

(The CRACK HO STRIPPER STRIPPER works it out with nasty choreography!)

and then all of a sudden she goes… *(Music cuts out abruptly.)*

CRACK HO STRIPPER: Damn, Muthafucka whatchu got on!

JAY: Well I had on a Calvin Klein T-shirt, Marithe and François Girbaud jeans, and my Gaultier belt. This was the early Nineties! I loved big-buckled belts.

CRACK HO STRIPPER: Muthafucka that shit hurt. Don't be coming up in here with some big-ass belt on. But if you do come up here with some big-ass belt on muthafucka, you betta use it! But it's gonna cost ya! *(Pause.)* Damn! Who let this cheap "bougie" muthafucka with the big-ass belt on come up in through here, bustin' my coochie!

JAY: I was so embarrassed. So I said, Rick, please can we go to the bar and get a drink, better yet, let's go outside for a while please, I need some air.

RICK: A'ight, A'ight…

JAY: Rick, there is something I gotta tell you. I guess there really is no time like the present. Big Brother, I'm about to take a big step with you here. And he's like,

RICK: What? What?

JAY: I can't believe it! I just blurted it out. RICK I'M GAY! Now, I had no intention of coming out at this moment but with the crack ho stripper, dill pickle and all – well I just couldn't help myself.

RICK: You're what?

JAY: I said…I'm gay!

RICK: Like a three-dollar bill?

JAY: I guess.

RICK: As a Christmas tree?

JAY: I guess.

RICK: Like cousin Siferdean?

JAY: *(Emphatically.)* Hell NO! I mean yes! I mean no! I mean kinda.

RICK: You are?

JAY: *(Nervously.)* Yeah.

RICK: I don't care, man, I love you anyway.

JAY: And of course I'm like AWWWWW! I am bawling, I mean Telemundo novella bawling.

RICK: Yo. Brother, I'm honored you feel that you can trust me. Don't worry, man. This is just between you and me.

(Pause.)

JAY: Anyway! A week later my sister calls…

AVERIE: Jay, me and Rick were on the phone the other night…

RICK: So, Ave, what if you found out that somebody you knew was gay?

AVERIE: I know somebody gay?

RICK: I'm just saying what if?

AVERIE: Who? Who?

RICK: I'm just saying…

AVERIE: Is it Phillip Lamar? Michelle? Who?

RICK: I promised not to tell.

AVERIE: Kareem?

RICK: No.

AVE: Someone at church?

RICK: What?

AVERIE: The Entire Men's Choir! I knew it!

RICK: No.

AVERIE: Cousin Siferdean?

RICK: We all know that. But you're getting warm.

AVERIE: It's a relative!!!

RICK: It's someone really, really close!

(Pause.)

AVERIE: *(Mouths.)* Someone really, really close?
(After some thought.) NOOOOOO!!!

RICK: Ummm hmmmm!

AVERIE: *(On the phone.)* Jay, *(Takes drag of
cigarette.)* I am really pissed off with you, I
can't believe it! I just can't believe it.

JAY: Listen Averie. I'm sorry if you can't deal
with it but, this is something that I have been
struggling with for years.

AVERIE: Unh Unh, I thought we were close!!!
I can't believe that you would tell Rick first.
(Take a drag of cigarette.) Listen, Gay Gay, I'm
cool with it, but I just think that you should
tell Mom and Pop. They shouldn't hear this
kind of news second-hand. Like I did!!!

JAY: So I thought about it. I had hidden that part
from my family. I hid from myself and there
was no way to continue thanks to Rick and
the Crack Ho stripper. So, I just went for it, I
called my mother. Mommy, uh Mom, I've got
something really important I want to talk to
you about.

EDIE: What? What's Wrong?

JAY: Nothing's wrong.

EDIE: What? You need Money?

JAY: No.

EDIE: Are you in some kind of trouble? What happened? Oh Lord, you ain't in jail are you?

JAY: Mom…

EDIE: What? Did the Student Loan people find you?

JAY: No, Mom.

EDIE: You got somebody pregnant!!!

JAY: No, No, No!!!

EDIE: What's wrong, Baby?

JAY: Mom, I'm gay.

(Beat.)

EDIE: Child, you so silly, would you be for real. *(Laughs.)*

JAY: *(Laughs.)* Mom, I'm serious. I'm gay.

EDIE: G...G...G? Well, um, you know, ugh, Siferdean was, um well you know...you know he wore scarves and things, you don't wear scarves and things do you?

JAY: Sometimes.

EDIE: Lawd have mercy!

JAY: Mom I'm just kidding.

EDIE: *(Sigh of relief.)* Oh, ok.

JAY: Only to church!

EDIE: Oh Lawd!

JAY: Mom, I'm kidding!

EDIE: Boy this is no time for jokes. *(Thinking.)* Whew. Mmm, mmm, mmmph. Jay Jay, You're my son. There is nothing that you can tell me that would make me stop loving you, only maybe if you said that you were a serial killer or something like that. Lawd have mercy! *(Secretly.)* You know, I can't tell your stepfather this! This will have to stay between you and me, alright son.

JAY: O.K. Mom. *(Pause.)* ANYWAY, 20 minutes later I get a phone call.

EDIE: Jay?

JAY: Yeah, Mom?

EDIE: I wanted to tell you… I talked to your stepfather about what we talked about?

JAY: Really? What did he say?

EDIE: Hold on…

POP: Jay?

JAY: *(Voice is pitched hi to very low.)* YEAH? Yeah? Yeah? Hey how you doing Pop,

POP: Well uh, yeah! You know what me and your mom talked about? Yeah. Well. I just want you to know that, you're a good boy, you're my son, maybe not by blood but you are my son. So it's cool, it's cool. You don't wear scarves and thangs do you? Something about that just don't look right on a big-ass man. *(Offstage.)* Sit down Edie! *(Back to Jay.)* But love is love right?

JAY: Right.

POP: And just so you know son, this conversation won't go any further!

JAY: And he never spoke about it again. He didn't have to! His Teddy said it all!

(Listens to Teddy Pendergrass reprise cue.)

After cleaning the house, I left the many
crates of albums down in the basement. I
figured I would come back to get the rest of
albums. I took a few of the old records with
me and went to visit my parents in Virginia.
My parents were going through some tough
times and I thought, maybe this will inspire
some dancing and good times like the time
that me and my sister performed the "robot
and the bump" to thunderous applause at
Aunt Thelma's Fish Fry. But then Cousin
Margo got pissy drunk and cussed out Cousin
Noni and snatched off her wig and pushed her
down a flight of stairs and…

Anyway, I needed to go see my parents
because my stepfather Clarence had what my
siblings and I believed was a fake heart attack.
I'll explain. You see my mother was diagnosed
with Lupus and then on top of that Leukemia!
And we all believed that Clarence's passing
out on the living room floor clutching his
heart was just a sad and desperate cry for
attention. I'll explain.

For months, anytime Mom spoke of an
ailment, Pop seemed to have been challenged
for attention about his ailments, including his
dialysis treatment, backaches, poor eyesight,
gas, hair follicle stress, and anal seepage.
You could not match a malady to Pops for
he was sure to top you with a full descriptive

63

rendition that would finish with a violin and a tissue. He was in the hospital and the doctors were running tests to find out exactly what was wrong. Did he have a heart attack? Or was he just obsessed with being the loudest, most dramatic black man on the East Coast? He was slightly conscious telling my mother stories of the "other side".

(Music cue: Lou Rawls "You're Gonna Miss My Loving".)

According to Pop, God looked like Lou Rawls and he was wearing a three-piece white linen suit with a gold fedora. *(Music out.)*

To be fair, with my Pop's diet of anything fried, his likelihood of having a real live heart attack was as common as Aretha Franklin wearing something that she know she shouldn't. So it was time to scrape up some money to go to Petersburg, Virginia to check on Clarence and Edie.

I took the Amtrak train and agreed to meet my sister and her seven-month-old baby girl, Jalicious. She and the baby Jalicious would hop on the train at 30th Street Station in Philly and we would continue down south.

(Music cue: "Square Biz".)

My sister arrived blasting her mini boom box and swigging a tall boy of St. Ives, while cradling her suckling with barrettes way too large for her teaspoon of hair. My sister's hair on the other hand was curled hard, pressed, layered, stacked, dookey braided, weaved, baby hair slicked, Kool Aid Red and dripping with paraphernalia. A Philly Creation! I was mortified! She sat down next to me and said to me, ever so intimately

AVERIE: I'mma get my drank on! For real!!! I don't know about you but we gonna need some liquor for this trip. Your cheap-ass brother Rick is going to catch the Greyhound. Say that shit is going to take 10 fuckin' hours. He'll spend $200 on some Filas and he won't shell out some money on a ticket for a Choo Choo. I ain't trying to ride the bus with people that's gonna get on my gat-dammed nerves and I can't move, what!???

JAY: My sister, the baby Jalicious and I were greeted by my mom who I thought looked much smaller than I remembered since six months ago and next to her, an ebullient 6 foot 2, Aunt Juanita my pop's sister. Aunt Nita looked as big as a house. Now – I am not sizist but she eclipsed the doorway of the train station. She was gathered in a complete southern gone to meet the relative's ensemble. All pink. Pink Hat, Pink jewelry, Pink dress,

Pink stockings, Pink scarf, Pink, Pink, Pink!
The only things that weren't pink were her
house shoes, which were tan men's sneakers
with the backs cut off and the sides were cut
out to give her painfully aching bunions a sigh
of relief.

AUNT NITA: There He!!! There He!! There's you
boy Edie!!!

MOM: Lawd, son have you been eating, always so
skinny.

AUNT NITA: Always a little bitty thang. Hey
Boy. Averie he he he – Look at that Hair!
Wonderful.

AVERIE: Thank you! Jay wouldn't let me cornrow
his hair!

JAY: *(Scoffs.)* Hi Mommy. Aunt Nita you looking
good, have you lost some weight? Looking
like Halle Berry!

AUNT NITA: Halle Berry? You don't gotta blow
no sunshine up my rear, I know I'm big as
hell! Look how handsome you've gotten.
Looking like Eddie Murphy. Don't he look
like Eddie Murphy, Edie? Looking so manly!
Gimme some sugar!

AVERIE: Give her some sugar Jay! I know you
got some sugar to SPARE! *(She mouths.)* Like

that one? *(She enjoys this.)* Mom what's up under that wig you wearin'?

EDIE: Oh lawd chile, that chemo has been tearin' me up! I've got about as much as that babies? About this much! *(She snaps her finger.)* Look at my beautiful grand baby. I'm so happy that y'all came down. Thank you. My children. Averie? Where's Ricky?

AVERIE: Don't get me started. He took the Greyhound!

EDIE: Oh Lawd. He ain't never gonna get here!

AUNT NITA: Well come on ya'll! Your father is half dead, chile, we better get on over to that hospital.

(Music cue: Smokey Robinson's "Cruisin".)

JAY: Driving in Aunt Nita's Ford Granada was an experience. As she turned the ignition the tape player pumped out Aunt Nita's favorite classic Smokey.

After some squeals of the engine she put her sized 11 house shoe to the metal. That heifer can tear through some rubber. As we peeled out of the parking lot, Mom gave a few Whews! And Lawd Nita's!!! Trying unsuccessfully to persuade Aunt Juanita to slow THE FUCK DOWN!!! *(Music fade out.)*

My pop was sitting up in his hospital bed,
very energetic, eating a turkey burger with no
bun.

The greatest concern at the moment was
that my pop was now suffering from a little
confusion. He was telling crazy-ass stories.
He believed that he was twenty-five and he
was living in Texas. The doctors were very
concerned because they said that they had
no idea what was wrong and why he was
delusional. Maybe he lost some oxygen when
he was passed out on the floor. Maybe a slight
stroke. They would run a series of tests. My
sister's medical diagnosis was –

AVERIE: He's just trippin!

JAY: After finishing his turkey burger with no
bun, he focused his gaze on Edie.

CLARENCE: I'm going over to that man's house
to kick some ass, and then Jerome and I are
going to pick up some money and a new car
in Atlantic City.

EDIE: Clarence what are you talking about, I
don't understand. And what's all this about
Lou Rawls. Now, Clarence I know he was
a good singer but you know that man ain't
God!!!

CLARENCE: DON'T YOU CONTRADICT ME!
I seen you. I seen you. I know you are out
running around on me. Running around with
that man. I can smell him on your breath.
You betta leave that man alone. I'll leave you
before you leave me! I'll leave you before you
leave me!

EDIE: Clarence calm down, you know I'll never
leave you; I would never be with someone
else. I love you, honey.

JAY: With that, I love you honey, Pop suddenly
jumped up out of the hospital bed and for the
first time I saw my pop's very unattractive
saggy ass through the hateful paper-thin
gown. My sister Averie busted out laughing,
Aunt Nita gave a "Jesus Clarence!" I called
the Nurse! Nurse! Two very strong young
white nurses came rushing in (I think that they
were twins, very surreal!) and they coaxed
my pop back to the bed. My mother's face
showed every second of her 63 years. My pop
continued his babble of I'll leave you before
you leave me, I'll leave you before you leave
me! Or was it babble?

Mom seemed to decipher Pop's lunacy like
she knew the key to his ancient hieroglyphics.
She stroked Pop's head and whispered –

EDIE: I'm not going anywhere, I'm not going
anywhere honey.

JAY: I began to realize that maybe this wasn't babble after all.

(Music cue: Gladys Knight and The Pips "The Best Thing That Ever Happened".)

Maybe, my pop a strong black man didn't have a way to cope with my mother's diagnosis. Instead maybe he desperately wanted to leave this earth, before the woman that he loved grew more ill and he was left to deal with the deck that he had been dealt. Maybe he didn't think he was strong enough to make it without her. Maybe, that fictitious man she was running around with was her maker and he was on her breath, on her lips and Pop could taste it. Or maybe I'm just a hopeless romantic trying to make sense of chaos. My mom shh'ed my pop. She said,

EDIE: Sing with me Clarence. Come on honey. Like you used to!

(EDIE begins to sing the line from the lyric "If any one" inserting a personal text plea to CLARENCE "You know this song" then the other half of the lyric "should ever write,my life story" then she says "You used to sing this with me all the time." This becomes a duet of text and music. GLADYS becoming EDIE's voice and CLARENCE singing with her. CLARENCE haltingly sings the next line in the song. Then he says -)

CLARENCE: Edie I don't feel like singing no song.

(But then the song seeps into his pores and he haltingly sings the next phrase. He begins to enjoy it. He sings the chorus of the song. He loves this one. It is the love story of him and his wife.)

EDIE: Thank you honey. You're the best thing that has ever happened to me too.

(Music swells and CLARENCE takes over the next verse. EDIE slips this text in as he sings.)

EDIE: I love you Clarence.

(CLARENCE's singing is pained and filled with the realization that he may lose his wife and how much she means to him. It is a battle of emotion of letting the big strong black man actually feel. It is explosive in song. He finishes the rest of the song, tears streaming down his face. Shaken. Inserting his wife Edie's name before the last line of the song. The song fades. Silence.)

JAY: So, Pop recovered. The diagnosis <u>was</u> a heart attack. Brought on by poor diet, stress and from what the psychologist could determine, depression. His delusions were still under scrutiny. My brother Rick finally showed up 13 hours later on Greyhound. And Averie, the baby Jalicious and I would leave a few days later. We all helped around the house and tried to get my mother to slow down. When you get older, it seems you sleep less and try to keep as busy as possible. Try to get things in order, try to get things done, before it is all over. Averie, Rick, the baby Jalicious and I took the train back up North.

JAY: Ave, please don't put that boom box on I don't want to get kicked off this train!

AVERIE: Shut up. I'll keep it low. We need some traveling music.

(Music cue: The O'Jay's "A Family Reunion")

AVERIE: Oooh that's my song! Jay, now explain to me why you are going to stop off to see that old-ass house on Chancellor Street?

JAY: We have to get the rest of those records out before the new owners take over!

RICK: Damn, this is the JOINT! AMTRAK! This is LIVE!!!

AVERIE: Told you! Cheap ass DOG!

RICK: I love you too!

AVERIE: Quiet! Don't wake Ja'Re!

JAY: You mean Jalicious?

AVERIE: Ja'Re is her name fool. You really took me seriously when I told you that I named her Jalicious. I ain't that Ghetto!

JAY: Well that's what everyone calls her!

AVERIE: Her nickname fool!

JAY: Anyway, I thought it would be nice to say our farewell to our nest.

RICK: That is so gay.

JAY: No it's not! Don't y'all care that the house is not going to be ours anymore?

AVE: It's just a house. NO!

(She sings the opening verse of "Family Reunion". After the second line she inserts an off-handed but loving comment to Rick, "Even you black dog!")

(JAY turns down the music.)

JAY: Rick, that house won't be ours anymore. I don't know why it bothers me so much but they left all those records behind! Those records were our life.

RICK: Records were our life? That is so…

JAY: I know, I know, GAY!

RICK: Naw. so sweet! That is so sweet little brother. *(Beat, then RICK sings a little with the O'Jays, A Family Reunion (twice) then –)* When did they get so old lil brother?

JAY: What? The records?

RICK: Naw, man, Mom and Pop! Did you take a look at Mom's hands? Or Pop's eyes? *(Beat.)* You know, I bet Mom and Pop left that music down there on purpose! They musta wanted some other family that moved in there to enjoy 'em as much as we did.

AVERIE: Unh unh unh unh unh!? *(Lip Pop)* Mom and Pop went out to Virgin Records and got all that old stuff on CDs a LONG time ago! What?!

RICK: Little brother I know that the house being sold for you is real deep. But you know we have to let go of the past to move into the future. Whatever it may hold. Maybe this music can help remind us who we are and what we are about? Especially now, dealing with Mom and Pop getting older, in and out of the hospital. *(Pause.)* Don't worry man. Things are going to be the way they are going to be. So maybe you should go and get those records and keep the records and keep the soul! Take it Ave.

AVERIE: A family reunion. Do it Rick!

RICK: A family reunion. Do it Jay!

JAY: No. No we're going to get kicked off this
    train!

AVERIE: It's so nice *(Lip Pop)* to come together

RICK: Come together

JAY: Get together! *(He laughs.)* We're going to get
    kicked off of this train.

(Music fades out like a memory.)

JAY: My sister, Averie, made me a mixed tape to
    send me on my way. Who does that anymore?
    A mixed tape! She made a mixed tape of a lot
    of the music that filled our home.

*(Music cue: The Jackson's "Show You The Way To
Go".)*

JAY: I finally did get back to the old house. I got
    a few records out and I left a few. My mind
    spinning. Trying to prepare myself for the
    inevitable. Like, childhood houses being sold
    and letting go of the things that you hold dear
    with a hope that they will still be a part of
    you. Let me show you. Let me show you the
    way to go. I can still hear the soul pouring out
    of our house. A year after the house was sold,
    I made sure that the obituary for Pop read like
    liner notes to his favorite album. I would go
    back, stand outside of that house and listen.
    A few months later, when Mom was laid to

rest, I made sure that she wore her white suit with the Dolman sleeves just like the one that Diana Ross wore in my favorite movie *Mahogany*! I went back to the house to listen.

Let me show you. Let me show you the way to go.

EDIE: Keep a song in your heart and you will always find your way!

JAY: *(Sings.) Let me show you. Let me show you the way to go.* When you are a kid you have no idea what these phrases that parents shell out by the dozens mean. With adult eyes, I realize that, that is how they made it through hard times. Keeping songs in their hearts. And you know that there are times as you make your way in the world that you muster up every ounce of strength to do just that. You feel like giving up and giving in. Or as my sister Averie put it –

AVERIE: *(Lip Pop)* Like the other side of the 45! Side B!

JAY: But you gotta, Keep the records, Keep the Soul.

EDIE: Keep the records, Keep the Soul.

CLARENCE: Yeah son, Keep the records, Keep the Soul.

RICK: Yeah little brother, Keep the records, Keep the Soul.

(JAY looks back at the basement. A memory.)

JAY: I got everything out of that house I needed. I could let it go. I would keep the soul.

He steps into that memory and pulls out a classic Donny Hathaway vinyl album.

All of my records to keep on moving. Spin them together like the ultimate DJ. Spinning till the end of never.

(Music out.)

It's called Soul Music. It gets into your body and takes you…

Music cue: Donny Hathaway that begins at the swell and phrase… "Keep on walking tall…hold your head up high." Ends with "Just wait and see some day we'll all be free."

WWW.OBERONBOOKS.COM